AF544655

Places of Comfort, Places of Justice

Places of Comfort,

Poems by
Christopher Bursk

Places of Justice

Humanities and Arts Press
1987

For June – what an honor to read with you, a poet of spirit + courage

May you + your work flourish

Chris B
MacDowell

This volume was selected by Lucille Clifton to receive the Schelby A. Sweeney & Courtney E. Cox Award for Creative Writing of the Creative Writing Program, San Jose State University.

Published by Humanities and Arts Press, San Jose State University School of the Humanities and the Arts Alumni Association, c/o English Department, San Jose State University, San Jose, California 95192.

1986-87 Editor: Naomi Clark

Some of the poems in this collection have appeared in some version in the following publications, to whose editors grateful acknowledgment is made: *Antioch Review, Encounter, I Know, Images, Manhattan Review, Massachusetts Review, Mildred, Painted Bride Quarterly, US 1 Worksheets, Poetry* ("Rowing Cutthroat Creek," "Sisters," "The Trees Keeping Their Places," and "After Being by Myself All Day"), and *The American Poetry Review* ("Vacation Bible School," previously titled "Red Cross Bloodmobile"). Also, "First Aid at 4 A.M." was originally published in "Place of Residence," Sparrow Poverty Pamphlet No. 44, Sparrow Press, 1983; and "Katherine, You Would Have Loved Your Own Wake" first appeared in the chapbook "Making Wings," State Street Press, 1983.

The author wishes to acknowledge a debt of gratitude also: "to my dearest teachers, Pamela Perkins-Frederick, Edward and Catherine Bursk, Christian, Nora, and Justin Bursk. Special thanks to the John Simon Guggenheim Foundation and the National Endowment for the Arts for grants providing me the time and confidence to finish this manuscript. And thanks to Ray Reilly, Bill Zalot, George Drew, Joseph Adzarito, and Elizabeth McCarthy for teaching me about courage."

Library of Congress Cataloging-in-Publication Data

Bursk, Christopher.
Places of comfort, places of justice.
I. Title.
PS3552.U765PS 1987 811'.54 87-16868

ISBN 0-9616835-1-1

Designed by Felicia Rice of Moving Parts Press, Santa Cruz, California
Manufactured in the United States of America

In memory of Katherine Adzarito, David Stoughton,
and Eleanor Wharton Atkinson ("Elf")
and
for Herb Perkins-Frederick and Bob Fraser
for A Woman's Place
and, above all, for Mary Ann

Foreword

As a judge of poetry manuscripts one is left finally with all that one has as a poet, one's naked self. My way of doing is to read every poem of every manuscript, afraid that I might otherwise miss some gem, some coming together. What I admire is courage, risktaking, respect for the music of the whole language and an intellectual and emotional stance. And honesty.

All that I admire came together for me in *Places of Comfort, Places of Justice*. The power of this manuscript sits in my mind even now. Reading it, I turned from judge into reader into poetry lover/fan. I congratulate its author.

Lucille Clifton
January, 1987

Contents

IV

I

Ice Fishing

For hours at this hole in the ice
the boy pretended to be the last person alive,
left with the task of testing the world's depths,
pulling up line, measuring by arm's lengths.
He'd feel the little tug
of the metal weight and then all the lovely looseness
of the line. This morning he'd heard his mother breaking dishes,
his father sobbing with anger again,
crying out, "For God's sake,
for God's sake, Kay."
He thought if he just tried hard enough,
did one thing well,
he might fix things, he'd bring home a fish
just as if he were a normal kid in a normal family,
and his mother would be so pleased, she'd get dressed,
the kitchen would fill with tarragon and butter
and fish sizzling, that luxurious oily smell,
and his father would open the windows at last,
and the winter air, sharp and clean,
would cut through the grease
of too much happiness.

Rowing Cutthroat Creek

I hate him, I hate him, Samuel told the oars,
the boat, the creek—he was rowing the black freight
of an old hurt he couldn't budge on land.
But afloat, there was nothing he couldn't slide forward.
I hate him, I hate him,
the arms thrusting before him
as if shoving a man against a wall,
jerking him back.

His father was the weight of the water
Samuel was pushing out of the way, the air
he was cutting, blade after blade. At home
his father was in the bread Samuel ate,
in the shadows on the walls, in the windows
Samuel wanted to break but didn't dare.
But here on the water, Samuel
could dip his blade in the man's body
again, again, get a rhythm to his rage,
let it propel him forward, nothing could stop him now,
make him feel stupid or small again.

And in the evening he could go back
and what had seemed heavy in his hands
would be light: hammer, axe, firewood, family bible
weightless in his hands. He had lifted the creek,
the sun flashing on his oars, water
had unraveled at his touch,
the face of the man was in the waves
and he broke it,
and the body of the man stretched out under him
and he moved over it.

Baseball Cards

All day I put off opening my last pack, the joy
of giving in to a secret pleasure,
the folds pulling away from each other, the paper breathing.
If I pressed and then released it,
the wrapper seemed to have its own life,
one curve lifting and lapsing into another.
I used to go home after school to Hall of Famers
I'd lured out of retirement, back-up catchers
and aging rookies coaxed over
from the Mexican Leagues. I'd taken cardboard backings
from my father's shirts, painted them green
and taped them so they could be folded away,
and when I rubbed the dice just so
between my palms, I was glad for another language, a world
where I didn't have to look busy at recess
tying a shoelace over and over.
The dice spilled on my diamond
and I covered them with my palm,
then slowly spread out my fingers, just wide enough
so I could read my fate there: fielder's choice,
sacrifice fly, single. Sure,
I was tempted to brush the board,
tip a die off its edge.
But when you play alone, honor's all you have,
all that gives the strike zone meaning,
each at-bat sending me to a page
in my rule book. The beauty of certain names hurt me,
Orestes Minoso, Luke Easter,
Paul Edison Miner.
It didn't matter to me what the card said:
6′5″, 201 lbs., 31 years old, a record of 6-17 for the '51 Cubs.
In his picture he was pale,
slender, even elfin,
and I gazed into his face
as if into a lake where the mist was burning off,
as if when the haze lifted
I might sink into the glimmerings there.

Shooting Baskets

The boy pries up the ice from the driveway
till there's blacktop and he's shooting
with one eye on the rim,
one on the window above him, the lamp there.
No, he doesn't really expect his Dad to put down his paper,
that tired, shy man, to come out into such cold,
or even to look down, wave.
But the dribble of a basketball
is the sound of a boy who won't give up,
who believes that if you perform the same act over and over
something wonderful happens.
In his games he starts hopelessly behind,
45-7, 62-13, 74-18,
and at half time kneels, draws shadow plays
on the little ice left. He's ashamed of the whole team,
how can they look anyone in the eyes after this?
And then it's all two-handed set-shots
from behind the trash barrels, sky hooks at garden's edge,
a fastbreak started at a snowdrift
and ending with his crashing
against the garage doors, the sag there
a kind of belly from where he's flung himself
many times before. Taking his own pass
he dribbles around ice patches,
one long stride into the air and across
and he's floating again towards the basket
as if he might lift like a curve forever.
Even in his jumpshot he's rising, his hand following
the ball's arc, reaching
after what he just let go. Each evening he listens
for that moment the ball drops
perfectly—not rolling around the rim and
rocking out, not even banked
off the backboard, but falling with the pure justice
he's waited for, the pleasure
of hearing—no, actually feeling—
from fifteen feet out, from thirty, in his fingertips
the swish, the ball jostling the strings.

It's that kind of sudden rightness,
an acknowledgement,
and he wants it again,
and in the little fragment of light
his father's lamp casts down
he shoots again and again and again.

Screwing

Screwing. It sounded deliberate, purposeful,
requiring a steady hand,
a mind moving over a thing, measuring, testing.
It's what a man did to fix things.
He tried to consider his penis as a screwdriver,
but even when it was firm
he couldn't imagine it pushing its way in,
the metal grooves opening the grain,
claiming hold there.
The best way for him to love a place
was to go naked in it,
press hard against all his father's things,
lathe, drill press, band saw table;
against an old, wide storm window,
stopping the darkness with his body, parts of him altering,
slurring against the glass.
What would other boys think if they caught him like this?
Hey, lead balls, did you get laid yet,
slip the old blade in the slot
and twist! They teased him
as if they wanted something from him,
as if he were a machine they were taking apart
and using words to do it: cunt, pecker, fuck, prick.
What would his father think?
Once from the slit of a just opened door
he'd watched his Dad nude
under the sun-lamp, turning slowly, a planet
shifting in its orbit,
a wrinkled geography, layers of dust.
Am I that different from other boys? he thought.
Touching a girl as they did
seemed impossible—a girl leaning over him, whispering?

She would call his penis *the Dagger*
and move her mouth along its shining blade.
Stabbed into her
how could it do anything but harm?
And then his penis was hard,

he held it like a joystick
as if attached to some awkward, makeshift machine
he was trying to get off the ground—
eventually he'd get this contraption to fly.

Did you get fucked, Sammy?
Did you finally stick the old pecker up the slot,
turn it for all its worth?
Better to be alone in the cellar's dusk, undressed,
moving among all that quieted, stabled power,
machines covered like expensive racehorses.
Better to be by himself, lifting his father's tools,
not to use them,
but to stroke, feel their weight: wirecutter, ratchet,
the brooding, aloof hammer, stalwart pliers,
best of all, the knurled brass screwdriver
whose bottom twisted open
at his grasp, blade slipped out of blade,
the tiniest as workable
as the largest, so many possibilities.
Better to lean against his father's worktable,
to press against the dark, heavy wood—
not to rock it back,
not to shift it off its feet,
but to feel it hold ground,
push back, to take the hardness into him
and for a few minutes be sure
the screws had been sunk deep enough,
things could be held together.

Kip to the Defense

Invite someone over, his mother says.
Why aren't you out with your friends? asks his Dad—
these classmates the boy's invented
to tell his family about in the silence
between pouring milk and drinking it. He takes pride
in making up stories on the spot, a friend's aunt
so drunk she peels tulip bulbs
instead of onions for his and Rog's hamburgers,
a girl whose skin's tinged blue, a boy with a clubfoot
who wakes up in far fields, having dreamed of flying.
Kip likes the challenge of taking the odd
and turning it ordinary.
There are no best friends in his stories,
he's careful to have kids move
before his mother can call their mothers.
One boy's Dad is being transferred,
another, Dougie, has no phone,
has to stay around to help his old man.
Sometimes Kip goes over even when Dougie's not home
to give Dougie's father a hand
chopping wood or lifting shingles up to the roof.
But how can a one-armed man shingle a roof?
his Dad asks. *He can't,* Kip says,
without me. The two of us have a system worked out
for wallpapering too. We're starting
on the kitchen tomorrow if it's all right with you.
Some evenings Kip has to risk
making himself his story's hero
and then he almost sees himself stepping forward,
ending his silence at school,
rescuing a boy even shyer than he is,
taking the punch intended for the kid and not flinching.
His fingers twist the napkin as he gets up now
from the supper table, his voice clear
and defiant. What else could he do?
he asks his Dad, but stand his ground
as he does here, in the kitchen, declaiming
without faltering, in one breath he's saved just for this moment.

The Ladies' Room

On rainy days when no one was at the Golf Club
my brother and I'd follow the old plaques
upstairs to the Ladies Room. Afraid to be caught
we'd go slowly, drawing out the fear,
listening with our fingers
on the railing. Then we were in the shadows
where Janet Hobbs had undressed,
Mrs. Gilman Churchill had showered,
and we imagined the pale inner thighs, the secret parts
of Lib Halvester, Sylvia Choate,
of Kit Waverly who chain smoked and broke par,
let her dress slip to the floor
worn now from women's bodies dripping,
their bare feet on towels.
We roamed the stalls, rubbing our hands
around each toilet's rim, ran the water softly
as if listening we might learn something new
of these ladies who dug their spikes into the greens.
We didn't know what else to do
in this room—had planned all kinds of pranks
with toilet paper, tampon grenades—
and now we were turned quiet, fidgety,
just as in church. Here
just as there we made little difference.
Here we ended up pissing in each toilet
and flushing.

"Unscrew the locks! Unscrew the doors from their jambs!"

Our teacher had taken off his jacket,
rolled up his shirtsleeves and was stretching out his arms
not to us exactly, but to that bright space
often between us and him at that time of the day,
a shaft of light and shifting particles of dust.
Look, our teacher said, *Why do we wear these things?*
and he made one boy undo his tie,
then another. He took off
and let his own long, silk tie loop around his hand,
through his fingers' webs,
across his wrist, pulled it slowly up his bare arm,
rubbed it along his cheek,
told us all to do the same. *Feel the tiny bristlings?*
Each of you is covered like this
with a fine, glistening fur. And his hand brushed across a boy's face—
one of our class who didn't shave yet—
and it was as if he'd touched us all.
How can I ask you to be brave if I'm not?
Then he was taking off his shirt,
and there were black hairs on his belly,
a terrible whiteness underneath, his two nipples.
We were scared for Mr. Bressler
and for ourselves, gripped the sides of our desks.
He went to the window high over the parking lot
and opened it. His shoes were off,
he was actually stepping out of his pants.
This should have been funny, a story
we'd tell our friends later
on the man we'd come to call *the Guru* or *the Old Homo*
at our lockers or waiting for our bus.
But now all I thought of doing was taking off my blazer—
didn't other kids want to, too,
get up, go to him, drape a coat over his shoulders
as he stood by the window, sobbing?
His penis seemed a mistake, a cruel deformity,
nodding, nodding, blunt and stupid.
There was too much nakedness for us to cover.
The boy next to me kept digging his nails into an eraser,

another fingered the crease of his pants,
a third let his hands drop to his ankles, the tip of a shoelace.
Who of us wasn't sick with fear, watching the clock,
the window, anywhere the man wasn't weeping,
disturbing the sunlit air?

Sexual Typology

It was Onan I turned to first,
at fifteen—son of Judah,
the one we skipped in Sunday School
though he was right smack in the middle
of the Joseph story, beating off.
Then sometimes I was Joseph, the strong, cruel fingers
of his older brothers on me.
I dreamed of being rescued from the pit,
a young Ishmaelite girl bathing my stinging wounds.
I was lying flat on a stone bed
and when her hand brushed lightly over my shoulder,
over the small of my back, my buttocks,
it was my hand, and now I was leaning over Joseph
careful not to press down too hard.
Would I always be a boy with queer, profitless dreams?
Not Joseph, not the one who grew bitter,
economist of dreams and seeds,
speculator in livestock and land titles,
but the youngest, Benjamin, proud once
to be a small shining next to such a brilliance,
permitted to gaze at a brother's nakedness,
the earnestness to each muscle,
the harmless, long back, the shoulders rising.
Benjamin, tending his father's sheep,
wondering what it'd be like to be seized
and stripped, traded for silver,
to be gloriously punished like Joseph,
to have his soft garments torn away too.
Alone I ripped my bedclothes from me,
I too, a brother magnificently wronged,
could hear the Ishmaelites whispering
as I lingered on the borders of a strange land.

His Father's Garden

Like God, his father has rarely changed his plans
and so the house is Samuel's at last,
and as soon as the family car has driven off
he's undressing, sipping dark rums, old clarets, imported brandies.
Far from town, there's no human now but he
with rights to everything,
the slope of the hill, the lake a mile off,
the moon the size of his fist.
He'll let the rain fall on him and stay as naked
as any flower, lift his arms slowly,
rise on the balls of his feet,
and then he'll sway to his own theories,
his heels landing where his father's hands had carefully planted
nasturtium, phlox, lilies of the valley.
What does a father know of his son's secret life?
Once in the men's department
Samuel had made his Dad and the store clerk wait
while, alone, inside a changing room,
he was stepping away from his underwear. He stood preening
in the glass, lifting on his toes,
twisting to see the buttocks' whiteness, the tilt
of the thigh, in the mirror a boy
motioning him closer with a curled finger, and he'd shone
in the bright glass, turned slowly,
bathed in his clear and hidden lake.
And now he'll sleep naked in the garden,
he'll tie his hand to his penis
so it'll stay stiff all night, there'll be someone else
fondling him—moonlight,
a shy sad woman, the tender elderly man
who'd whispered and stroked him on the bus once,
his skin white and slippery as petals.
Father, this is my garden, he sings,
I will live here forever.

Twin Necklaces

You wore my half of the universe
around your neck. On mine
the silver stars and the cracked moon
rattled like dog tags
when I showered. *Angel Face, Teen Angel, My Special Angel,*
all the songs I hummed into the pulsing water
were for you, as I rubbed the moon's
jagged edges, knowing
how perfectly it could slip back
into the grooves of its twin. And when boys teased me,
calling you Big Boobs, Wonder Womb,
I tore into them, ended up being tossed out the gym door
without even a towel.

She's too possessive.
She's just using you. She can't get any other dates.
She ought to take better care of her body.
My aunt was thin
and careful to say just enough to make you cry.
Now, Christopher, your girlfriend is just too sensitive.
Do you remember what ridiculous positions we got ourselves in,
how my mother found us
in the back cellar, on a blanket under the train table,
making out, as we called it then,
under the little town, the miniature metal people
in their proper places, station platform,
park benches, town square?
My mother pushed aside the entire park, schoolyard, town hall,
to get at us. Naked, we grabbed fields
and valleys to cover ourselves with.

It must have been soon after that
we drew up our suicide pact.
Arrested at a peace vigil,
I was to be sent off to military school,
the punishment having to fit the crime, my father said—
and the night before I was to go
you held a razor to your throat

and it was terrifying to be the only one
who could talk you out of dying,
and it was wonderful too.
That night we undressed in the dunes
and lay on our backs for a long while, not touching,
letting ourselves feel the ache of all that space,
that painful distance
that seemed the most important part of loving,
and it was you who caressed me first,
and when I took you in my arms
it was as if I were holding the sky,
its clear darkness,
an endlessness of fine, cool sand shifting under us.

Caressing

This is not love yet that gets her to stroke the stitches,
the small, pursed mouth of the anus,
to pull back the lobes of the buttocks
as if to say: I'm not scared of the shadows in you,
the long night within a young man's body.
She rolls him over,
rides him—he's naked as a wave
about to shatter
yielding himself—a gift he will offer up
not just to her, but to the dark around them
as if he really were a wave
that could never be made whole again.
And now she clings to him like the splintered hull of a boat,
pushes hard against him as if there's a storm,
the penis trapped
like a child caught between his parents as they clutch,
hold firm against a high wind.
And then she turns his face to hers
and then he's shuddering,
rocking against her, weeping,
there's too much grief, wave after wave breaking
and she's afraid
she can't be shore enough, it's as if a black ocean
were falling on her, the weight
of all his sorrow, exploding, his cry
of surprise, of sudden understanding.
He reaches out to touch her
as a survivor might caress the sand he's washed up on,
let it sift through his hands.
His fingers begin working,
he lays his head in the soft hollow
of her hipbone, gets as near as possible
as if leaning next to a safe, listening
for the tumblers, the secret combination.
She's a soft humming. So this is what it's like to be lovely.
Deep within her a woman,
one more beautiful than she'd ever imagined, is singing,
the tune faint at first,

she can just catch the rise and fall of the sound,
and then it gathers,
lifts with her like a wave.
She wants to stay like this: at the tip of cresting,
to listen for the crescendo,
feel the shadow before it is cast down.
She tries to hold back the song,
it surges within her like the music of the planets,
haunting, alien, terrifying,
she'll not be able to bear it any longer,
cannot keep herself from singing out.

Katherine, You Would Have Loved Your Own Wake

for Katherine Adzarito (1904-1984)

You'd have been up for hours before the caterers
baking treats, macaroons, meringues,
or slicing carrots thin so they curled, strips
soaked in the juice of mandarin oranges,
you who'd never had enough to eat as a child,
who'd put salt on your brothers' abandoned potato skins,
finished your sister's milk,
sucked your father's grapefruit down to its white pulp,
a woman who loved parties for the pleasure of working
on her own time, trading recipes,
making lists, buying new tablecloths, ordering flowers—
better to have too much
than too little, platters of spiced ham, pickle roll,
mortadella, three bean salad
to send afterwards to the neighbors, to Tiny and Geneva,
to Mary Fiore, to the Paulettes.
After guests left, you'd let the house grow dark around us,
as we put off the dishes—
you liked the time just afterwards, saying again
what had been said, not to understand
as much as to keep the wonder of it still in our voices.
But it was the day of a party I loved best,
the purpose to our work, getting ready,
the tools I was trusted with, radiator brush,
black toilet brush with the dip
that followed the pipes' deep curves into the house.
By late in the day, washing the moldings,
we'd squat down and get up suddenly
just to be lightheaded, giggling, gripping each other's sleeves
falling back. No one could rush you—not the late hour,
not even the doorbell, the first guests,
and I stood guard as you shed clothes
and ran for the steaming water I'd drawn. Downstairs
neighbors filled the rooms, the poker club, Father Tripodi,
the man from the post office
whom you'd baked cookies for when his wife died,

the girls from your floor at the shoe factory,
Cal Parino, his bad leg still bothering him,
Dr. Sullivan, Jimmy the Bookie and his wife
who owned the school bus company,
your best friend Nettie Durso, her sister Jenny Timpani, Phil
and Sil Fazio, even the paperboy
you'd been teaching not to be afraid
of a curve ball, to step right into it
and swing. How long ago was it
that I'd bring your guests sherry and apologies,
stalling for time while upstairs
you sank into the fragrance of lilac, into so much softness
touching you everywhere
you were considering never rising from it?
When would these people give up and go home,
leave the house shining and ours?

II

The Two Princes of Azarth

1

Seeing mother restless,
we offer to get her brushes and oils,
to pose for her.
Or we could clean the kitchen drawers,
the pastry brushes stiff with eggwhite glaze,
bulb baster with its juices dried to the glass stem.
We'd line up each crimper and wheel
by size and use.
Or what if we went for a walk,
one of those long ones
where you draw a line from home to anywhere
that sounds mysterious, Needle Rock,
Lost Sheep Pasture, Bound Brook,
and we take all day getting there
for the good exhaustion coming back?
What if we weed or plant bulbs?
Nothing we suggest today pleases our mother.
Soon, in just a few minutes,
we'll do something wrong,
hate ourselves for being so clumsy.
And then she'll scratch one of us.
It's always a surprise, like watching fire burn closer,
closer, but never really believing it'll leap up,
sink its claws in.
We can't count on our mother to let go of this rage
any more than we might trust fire
to worry, to stop
and apologize.
Now you've done it.
Now you've pushed me too far.

2

Weeks before mother's going to be taken from us again
we know, come home from school,
and slip the scissors from her fingers,
hide father's slashed dress pants,
the sleeves and shreds of his smoking jacket.
Or we tell her how we like the house this way,
empty and clean,
and then drag what we can of the furniture back inside,
off the curb. One day
we can smell rosewater and gardenias in her bedroom,
we listen to her determined humming,
the small sculptor's hammer
as she breaks one window, then another,
vials of perfume,
picture frames.
Afterwards we gather the brittle, curled leaves,
the petals of glass.

3

Any day now she'll be coming home,
you tell the women at the door, those who stare
as if we were the ones responsible
for sending our mother away. Some mornings
you have us circle back from the bus-stop,
let ourselves in the house
as soon as our father drives away.
Even after he's left, his silence
is like a sentence passed down upon us,
never to be revoked. I hold out my wrists
and you bind them, you make the cords especially taut
so I'll have something to pull against,
know the game's earnest.
And now the house's not empty,
the curtains are alive
with conspiracies. A candle-flame
singes the hairs of my legs, then the melting wax,
its little stingings,
and always at first it's silly, I'm laughing,
almost embarrassed at my pain. *Don't*
let them break you. Don't cry,
you whisper as you lean over me.
Our days now shall be filled with great wrongs done us,
long struggles to free our wrists.
If there's to be terror
you will have it of your own choosing,
you deciding, brother,
how much we can endure.
Here, in Azarth,
in the tower, you've been allowed inside all of history,
weighed down with its chains,
you feel light, exotic. It's a privilege
from a high window to watch the town's women
building up straw around the stake,
bending and curving the thin branches,
working like small grey birds

weaving a nest.
This is what you have waited for:
to be the subject of a formal ceremony,
at the stake, pale and solemn,
to speak deliberately and know everyone is listening,
for once in your life to be sure to be heard.

4

We can't trust anyone.
You make me swear to tell no one where we've been,
especially not father.
At school I have to think up excuses
when kids ask me to come over to their houses and play.
Their mothers are just putting them up to it,
they just feel sorry for you,
you insist. And if someone's at the door,
My brother's too sick, you tell them.
He's got too much work. If we don't get our chores done,
we'll be killed, you know how our father is.

5

Some nights you wake me and tell me what you've seen
happen to me, to you. There's a knife,
a rope, a window. *Go back to sleep. Dream it. Try to*
dream it with me, you whisper. Sometimes
when we don't have enough money for the movies
you get me to lie under the covers
with you. *Now dream,*
you command. I pretend
I don't notice you slipping letters up my pajama sleeves,
messages in silver ink
you'll say I've brought back from Azarth,
from your severe lords, Nisthar, Cyndril,
names that smell of smoke
in the curtains, in the old books in the attic.
There are strange watery syllables I can't read
but as soon as your hands are on them
you're translating. There are gifts you've left
to bring with us into sleep: a brass weeping bowl,
mother's cameo brooch,
an antique dagger.
Waking, you rise from your dreams with the same defiance
you meet the harsh sun with after a matinee.
Even though your hands are empty,
you insist I touch the dust of jewels there.
A man led you to a high chamber where the sun glittered
and he dressed you in silk
that felt as if you were wearing the light itself.
You've returned only for my sake,
make me feel the broken parts of your body,
make me confess whose grip
I tore myself from, what I sacrificed
to come back to you.

6

Whose world are we in now?
Whose hands are on us?
In our room there's candelight
and water we run quietly, dipping our fingers
into it. You have me pull the blinds,
you light the wick,
and we have the flame, that nimble, goat-footed boy,
that naked messenger
you can send tipping off the pedestal.
You bring him so close to your face,
you are almost kissing him.

7

Has it been a year since mother was light
and loose in our embrace,
since we had to hurry home to save a puppet,
one of her antique dolls, our toys,
to pry her fingers from the cat's fur?
And when she'd slumped to the floor,
I'd helped you lift her so when father drove up,
she'd look only a little dazed, a little sleepy
leaning between us. And now she's home
just for a visit, father tells us.
And when we are called down to say goodbye,
you don't let me go, even to the top of the stairs.
Even when father presses against our door
and pleads with you just to come to the window
and wave, you won't.
Not till you hear the car doors shut, the car pull away,
do you look out. Then you make me watch
as you thrust your fist through the window,
as the glass falls away in a family of cries.
You stretch your arm out
not to touch anything, but as if to salute,
as if you had to hold it there, stiff,
to stay at this terrible attention,
and though no sound rises from your lips,
I know what you are asking:
to put my hand through the window too,
reach into the same piercing hurt.

8

While you nap, I go to the kitchen
and draw out a thin, strong knife,
sharpen it so it'll slide softly in, mercifully
move through the muscle. I stand over you,
lying in your clothes on the bed,
too eager to enter your dreams to have undressed,
your hand on the staff
you'd carved for you to carry into Azarth.
Yesterday, awakening,
you had told me of the armor lifted gently off you,
of how you were led down a long corridor
to a hall bright with candles along its high walls.
If you had died then
you'd have had an easy passing, slipping
from one brilliant kingdom
into another. You'd have felt nothing
if the dagger were quick.
And now I feel the blade dipping under the wings
of your back, the surprise
of the skin slitting, the knife sinking
as if summoned,
searching deeper. I've done it.
I hold the knife to the window, amazed
at how clean the blade is. It seems a terrible accident
that I've imagined such an act
and done it.
And then an even more wondrous accident
that I have not.

9

I listen for the little static of your silks.
You are dressed like the night sky
and lead me away, blindfolded. The floor tilts
and I set down each foot hard, draw air
deep inside me, hold it
as if each breath were a level place I might move across.
You help me onto the windowsill.
How far can you get me to teeter back,
fling my arms behind me?
I'm permitted to grip only with my ankles
locked and pushing
against the inner wall. *Trust me.*
Lean back, Samuel. More.
Farther back. Lean even farther.
The wind on my shoulders is dry and cool.
Soon I'll drop away,
there'll be nothing to stop me.
I'll be falling out of this life
as you've wanted me to. There'll be only your hands
reaching out, your hands
to catch me.

III

Sisters

Upset with your father's letter, his anger
at you for hiring detectives to search for your sister,
you drive your car as far away
as your lunchbreak lets you,
park on the soft shoulder of River Road,
bend over your notebook
as if peering through a dusty skylight
into a deserted house, nudging open the window,
letting yourself down into the hall—
for every step there's an echo.
All the furniture has been left as it was,
the rosewood chest, the bevelled cabinet,
your father's wide desk,
the fluted, laurel-wreathed woodwork you rub the dust off.
Now you feel at your side a rustling
nightgown, your sister, shy and severe
as she's always been, escaped
from the upper room, voiceless, pale, almost invisible.
What could she have done to be so terribly punished?
She's as thin as ever,
in her face a vague pain as if she were about to disappear
in some dim place in her mind. Why have you never
gathered her in your arms?
This is the only way you know how:
you open your notebook,
showing her page after page.
She cannot vanish now, you keep her with your words,
this is the only thing she will listen to,
these dark poems.

The Strangler

Once I'd taken a nylon stocking, one of my mother's
with an exotic name,
soft mocha, dusk, moonlight haze,
and pulled it over me so I could feel what it'd be like, my face
    anonymous
and blank as a kneecap.
The man must have had to work for the little air he took in,
it must've come filtered through the delicate weave
of the stocking, each breath
a quiet hissing like an old machine
that couldn't be turned off: implacable, tireless.
Perhaps while I was delivering my newspapers
he was lugging his sample case of encyclopedias
up three flights of a dim staircase.
I'd take a branch and twist and twist and it'd tear
finally apart, I could peel one ripped half
off the long threads of the other.
Was this how the bones of a woman broke?
She'd have no name,
come to the door with her nightgown slightly open,
her breasts pure cloud.
I'd always wondered what it'd be like
to reach into the air and grip a cloud,
squeeze and crush it.
All day this man must have sweated up stairs,
listening for the scraping of a chair
wedged against a door.
Then, as if offering herself freely, a girl would look out,
she would have a name, Melanie,
and breasts soft and shifting
in loose sky-blue fabric.
And then his hands were on her throat
and all the day's foul work was worth it.
And as I delivered my papers I took turns
dying and doing myself in,
breathing through his fine mesh,
or trembling in his grip
unsuspecting, innocent, undeserving.

The Trees Keeping Their Places

She had come back from the woods
carrying her dress over her outstretched arms
like a child rescued from the lake,
offered it up to her husband's mother.
No one had said anything,
they had hurried her to bed.

She'd be fine, they told themselves.
One afternoon she came down from her nap
with the porcelain doll she'd had from childhood,
its savaged hair,
in her limp hands its scalp bald, face smudged
from where she'd rubbed it over and over.

What unspeakable act had been committed
against her? What had driven her
to this? her husband
wanted to know. At night, after making love,
she'd sit up and watch
just as he was falling asleep.
He looked like a wounded deer, too stunned
to move, to care, and she'd place her hand
on his chest, where the throbbing was.

Sycamore, black willow, sourwood, poplar,
these old bachelors never told,
these old domestics who had served her husband's family well,
why she carried her rage into the woods again,
a knife that shimmered so brightly
anywhere she tilted it
it was silver, many broken pieces of a mirror.
Why not plunge it in?
It would shine,
it would carry the light into her,
it would be the one pure motion of her life.

Colleagues

I've always hated people like Sylvia who make fine distinctions
between loneliness and being alone.
The house empty, the children gone for the weekend,
I'm ridiculous, a middle-aged woman
twisting the frames of my glasses.
Should I reach for the phone,
dial for help?
Help for what. Being shallow, mediocre, cowardly?
For sitting on the hall stairs
with my son's airplane in my fingers,
my nails digging into its soft balsa wood?
Somewhere Sylvia is drawing her bath,
opening a book to the page she's carefully marked,
combing her hair in the lamplight.
As a child I hated her type,
even more than the girls who teased me all the time.
She read by herself at recess,
she broke up fights,
hummed in line, was goofy yet everyone liked her.
She even smiled at me, lofty and distant
like some benevolent moon.
One might as well have told the moon to go to hell.
I used to imagine tricking girls like her,
getting one accidentally to hurt me
so she'd regret it the rest of her life.
What if, now, I waited in the parking lot after work
and when Sylvia accelerated, just a little,
I'd step off the curb
right in front of her car, fall down screaming?
She'd be dazed,
too shaken even to call an ambulance,
she who'd been so capable. She'd visit me in the hospital,
write notes—even the handwriting full of tremblings—
but I'd say nothing.
She'd take to looking in the mirror, rubbing her face
with both hands, feeling the skin
slide over the skull,
she'd not be able to look away. *Bitch, bitch,* she'd whisper,

who'd never sworn before.
She wouldn't know whom she was talking to.
Two weeks later I'd find her wandering the neighborhood.
There'd be gale warnings,
the cars parked on Elm Street would shudder with the sudden gusts.
The wind would heave itself against the trees along Atlantic Avenue
as if to punish them
for bending, for bending, for nodding so agreeably,
for refusing to break.
I'd follow her down Nichols Road, then Ripley
where it crosses Beach Street.
She'd be standing on Cunningham's Bridge, the worst place
in town during a storm.
She'd be leaning towards the rushing current,
her body pressing against the railing,
not using her hands to hold on—
if the winds were going to carry her away, okay,
she'd not save herself.
And I'd come up to her,
reach out. The gusts would get stronger,
flinging the sea up against our legs.
We'd need to grip hold of each other
to keep from being swept away.

Rachel

The voices are attentive, they do my will,
they are like bees in a jar,
set loose, they sting—
harrying a scientist, confusing a Pentagon general.
Against nuclear weapons, I have my own ways.
At night I press my hands hard to my ears
and blood throbs. A storm rises on the horizon
and I wade out into the black waters,
meet what's coming towards me.
Or I dig my nails into my scalp
as if to pull the brain apart
like two halves of a dried fruit.

And then for weeks I can see into the future.
Listen, your son is in danger.
Lock the doors, keep your boy beside you,
stand over him when he sleeps.
If you see him struggling
for air, as if entangled in fabric,
all the sharp bones of his body, ankles, elbows
trying to rip himself free,
if you see him tearing at the air
as if to open a small hole in it
where he could breathe,
lift him to you. When I was little,
my brothers tied me up while I slept,
forced me into my father's duffel bag
and lowered me into a pit of snakes,
soft, bulbous heads
pushing against me, coils
stretching across me like long, muscular arms.
Even after I was lifted up,
I could feel the snakes
threading and unthreading in my brain.

Now they move and bump, buzz like bees. Listen,
sleep lightly. Leave a door open
between you and your boy. Do not leave him alone
for long. Even if you don't believe me,
even if you think I'm crazy.

Where Else Is There to Go?

Then it's quiet, like just after a storm,
and you are driving around.
It all makes sense as you head for the library.

Little sister, you say
and take her clenched hand, white and cool
as a shell.

Then there is no broken chair in your hand,
you are not standing behind your father and baby brother,
he does not smell of gasoline.
Your Dad's hand is not raised.

Oh, I'll love you,
you whisper, *I'll kiss the tips of your fingers.*
Her nails glint like little slipper shells.

When you were a boy, you'd go under the dark eaves
of water and it'd collapse on you
like a house demolished with you inside,
plaster crumbling, walls buckling.
But in the surf you could still stand up,
only your ears ringing—
while at home, anger broke against you
like glass, your father shouted, *How could you be so stupid?*

And now you draw the girl aside,
you do it so gently she doesn't realize
she's being led off to a window,
to your own special bright place among the books,
and you ease her hand down.

Look, here is a train,
it has tiny, silver tracks, just under my belt buckle.
You can make it go up and down.

Don't pull away, don't be afraid.
Imagine the sun's falling through the windows
of your dollhouse, that quiet,
that slanted light.
It's travelled all these miles to stroke your face,
your throat,
the thin, winnowy hair of your arms.

Hit and Run

I'd killed a dog
years ago. The impact was the same.
You'd think a boy would make a special sound,
something terrible,
not the dull thwock
like a rock being struck by a hammer—
like when a piece of gravel
spins off the tire from someone else's car
and spits up, cracks your windshield,
and you wonder, Why you, why now?
The rest I don't remember
except I didn't wash off the blood right away,
but stood in the garage
just touching it,
drawing a little whiskey from the bottle.

Did you ever think about the stone path
you and I and the rest of the kids worked for days to lay just right,
the summer your mother and I married?
I wanted something perfect for her
after what she'd suffered.
You and the other girls wading in the stream, choosing stones,
giggling as if it were finally all right
to be particular, to be little queens: *Not that one! This one!*
The boys lifting the heaviest of the stones
higher than they had to,
not to show off—I'm pretty sure of this—
but as if to make clear
they could bear anything asked of them.
It took three months. Then we built the porch,
kind of in honor of the path.

Suddenly I'm a murderer?
I never missed a day of work in all those years.

At least I'm trying to figure it out,
to understand it? But the boy is still dead. Look,
there's just this path
and it leads here.

Adjusting

When the class's asked to list their talents,
Thomas prints ADJUSTING
in capital letters. "There's nowhere I can't adjust."

Yeh, Gaelinda adds,
Nowhere, honey,
laughing her "fuck you" laugh.

And when Tommy confesses how much he likes being runner
for the Infirmary, his voice
suddenly boyish, serious
like a kid's when he's talking about baseball
and playing in the majors,

Gaelinda calls over to him, *Homeboy,*
I know you too well.
I know you from the streets.
Today she's not going to let him be anything but an inmate.
I'm good at fucking men over,
put that down on your list. Don't matter where I am,
I do my dance.

When she leaves, she balls up the assignment,
she makes many sharp edges,
many flat surfaces buckling in on each other.
The paper almost barks,
it's a small pack of dogs in her hand.
You think I got room in my cell for this shit?
Afterwards I stroke out the wrinkles.
I find that she's filled in all the blanks on the page,
she's signed her name in flowery spiralings
and swirls, and over the *i*
there's a small heart
and under the column *Obstacles to Developing Your Talent,*
in lovely, looping capitals
she's written *NONE.*

First Offender

Lucky for this good-looking boy
he's in Seg Wing now;
the officer in Intake, seeing him naked,
his sloped back, his thigh's white curve,
had the good sense to assign him to a single cell,
a kid who fills up looseleaf, copying
from the one weight lifting book in the prison library,
a seventeen-year-old whose pale body
refuses to harden completely, the long throat, soft, ashen face,
the brown eyes that darken
as if he expects even me to strike him.

What's that luscious child doing,
that mama's boy? As Peter lifts by himself,
a few men along the fence, at yard-out, laugh,
a couple of hard-timers point
to their crotches. *Hey, beauty, curl your fingers*
around this. Here's some iron
for you to pump.

How did he get himself in such a mess, he wonders.
He'd liked climbing into the dark
of other people's houses, standing in one place
and listening till he heard the shades lapping on the sills,
the tires on the wet pavement outside.
Once, seeing a car's shadow curving around the walls,
even its driver outlined,
he'd found himself waving as he had as a kid.

He'd been in ninth grade when his mother vanished.
The trouble had started then—his father,
drunk, used to force him into a chair.
Sometimes he struck him,
often he tied Peter's wrists behind him,
and made him pay attention
as he told how he had pushed away
the arms of the boy's mother, held her down.
And now she was doing it with anyone,

even niggers, his father had screamed.
Right this very moment you mother's doing it with niggers.

What if you fought back?
What the hell, imagine it, I coax. *What might have happened?*
But Peter says, *No,*
no, this is how it had to be, as he remembers it,
the man shouting, mocking him.

You think you're so smart?
What would you do? Peter snarls, but he's not waiting
for my answer, he's already going on
to tell me how after a beating
he was expected to stop crying immediately, to sit there
and acknowledge his father's justice
while his Dad lit a cigarette and inhaled,
long, slow drags
before he gripped Peter's wrist,
pried open his palm, and drawing fire
into the cigarette's tip, put it out on his son's hand.

I'd have needed a little leverage,
Peter says. Maybe he could have thrust his knees up,
maybe he could have
pressed this heavy, drunken man back,
and then maybe just as quickly, grasped him,
pulled him so close the man couldn't free his arms.
And now Peter's leaning into his story,

he is rubbing the table's rim, the dark, scarred wood,
pressing his fingertips down
as if he might feel beneath them the atoms'
furious energy—not the pretty boy anymore, the kid
who has to be locked up in a special cell,
but the naked figure
in his book's diagram, even the little known muscles
turned hard and reliable,
triceps brachii,

serratus anterior, teres major and *teres minor,*
gluteus medius, tensor fascia femoris,
and with his hands
with just his fingers he lifts his attacker into the air
and he will not let this man go till he's sorry,
till the man's weeping
and Peter's ready to fling him aside.

Crewcuts

Just before I was arrested
I remember thinking I should get a haircut,
and needing something to focus on besides the sirens,
I closed my eyes and imagined the scissors, a silvery bird
pecking at me. I was an old nest
it was tidying up, a thicket it was picking at for sweet bugs.
The scissors moved in the air just over me.

I remember crewcuts. My mother made me and my brothers get them.
We loved the moment just after
running our hands across the bristles,
all those hairs at military attention. Then, older,
we could ask for more:
the barber would rub stick-um at the front tip,
put a slight curl to the first hairs.
That was the only place we needed to run a comb through
and we combed and combed,
glad to have something a bit stylish about us,
a reason to look in the mirror.
We'd come from a haircut
as if nothing in the world could beat us,
we were that sweet-smelling,
that sharp, as if bringing home something special
to show our mother, a treat
for her to touch and sigh over.

And now I can imagine how my mother would have felt
if she'd been there to see me lie down
on the streets still damp from the rain.
She'd have been almost as concerned about my long hair
as about my being arrested,
as if both rebellions would lead me to trouble too foreign
for her to protect me from. We were a few old women, several
    middle-aged men,
and some college kids trying to stop jeeps and trucks
with their dangerous cargo and singing
to the soldiers. We must have looked a raggedy row of bodies
like pictures of dead fowl laid out

to show how good the kill was.
Occasionally the wind lifted a scarf or a coat flap
like a loose feather. We'd been waiting for so long
we found ourselves almost hoping for the gas,
the clubs, the handcuffs.

In this county jail for the third time in his life,
my cellmate—twenty-two, here for petty theft—
frets with his hair. He's trying to keep it feathered,
can't stop it from flying off his forehead
like some broken wing that won't stay down.
Everyone can see he's damaged, knows
to peck at him, send him fluttering out of the way.
His mother has just died. One of the guards,
seeing his head hung down,
thinking he's just another man back from trial
facing hard time, just another
prisoner to be shipped from here,
laughs, pokes him in the chest,
Hey, Ferris, you look as if your old lady's
    been screwing behind your back.

Yeh, and yours fucks ducks.
That's all he's left, these insults
like wet matches he keeps trying to strike.
Just before, grief had been a cave
like the ones he explored as a child, kept secret,
where everything he said was to the wind at its mouth,
to the dark, disappearing emptiness inside.

He pushes his hands now through his thick hair
and makes both sides lift,
black straggly wings.
He'd given up showering, shampooing,
combing out the gnarls.
If they're going to treat you like a criminal
you might as well look like one.

And I think of my mother—dead now like Ferris's—
who knowing how little she could keep me safe from
put so much emphasis on a trim haircut,
well-groomed nails,
took such pleasure cutting my brother's and mine clean and perfect.

Today in the barber shop I know why my cellmate is crying.
It's unfair to have women here,
in jail, the female barber bringing in her special scissors
and combs, on her day off coming here
to teach the inmate trainees how to give the men a little style,
leaning over Ferris now,
touching his neck, cutting away
the soft curls of his raggedy hair.
Your mother is dead
and this is the only gift you know
to give her.

IV

Secret Gifts

Is your Dad in jail? Nora's teacher
had called across the room and the class had laughed.
Before I left home
my daughter warned me: I was to behave, this time,
I was not to get arrested.

And now we've taken the courthouse over.
None of us had believed the gas,
till we fell from it. One of the police
had grabbed a boy by his sweater,
another was bringing a club down on his skull
as we tore him away. A hundred of us have made it inside now,
guards set at the doors,
small groups of us telling the stories of our injuries over and over
as if somehow those who'd hurt us
could hear, like parents in another room
looking down at their hands.

Do you always have to get your name in the paper?
Nora's wanted me to be nothing but a father,
one who expects good grades,
rides bikes with her when her friends aren't around,
lets her tease,
comb the snarls out of his dark, straggly hair.
But here, waiting for the police to be sent in,
I find deep in my pockets
mints with sour jellies in their middles,
cashews, raisins she must have hidden in the good jacket
I always wear to get arrested—
two storebought cookies,
hers and my favorites.
As she'd do I loosen the sugar with my nails,
raise each crystal to the light.
It's a small magnificence.

Even the crumbs will do
and I begin searching the seams, along the threads,
into the sugary silt of my coat,

wetting my fingertips,
lifting to my tongue the dust of peppermint,
taste of salt.

Vigil

My son wants to know why one of the soldiers
is standing apart from the others. The young man's riot gear
hangs from his skinny body.
He puts his weight down on one foot,
then another. He shifts his club from hand to hand.
A woman's nursing her baby, one boy's in a wheelchair,
the rest of us get on our knees and sing
to make it harder for the soldiers.
They'll have to form a wedge and shove their way into our hymns,
our lullabies. Maybe one has a daughter
and he's been careful to tell her what she's a right to expect
from a man. But now he raises his club
as he might in a slow-pitch league, going to bunt,
and he thrusts it against a teenaged girl's breasts,
pushes her back. It's cruel
what we've driven these men to. A college boy's dragged away
by his hair. A man who's been leading our singing
stumbles. A few of the soldiers strike at him
as boys might, working in a field all day where the weeds
and tall grass keep refusing
to fall under a scythe. On either side
of the prison wall there's singing. We had agreed
at this hour, at the same time, today,
to lift our voices together. Thelma has passed the word
to the other inmates, this gentle, heavyset woman
whom I had to coax just a year ago to speak up
in class. My son begged
to be taken here, his love for Thelma
like his scorn for war
makes him feel adult, privileged.
How long do I dare stay here with this boy
who presses sleepily against me,
the age that still longs to be lifted
no matter who's looking,
no matter how far his legs dangle down?
What the fuck are you doing, bringing a kid here?
The young soldier tears my son's hand from mine,
and Justin is seized away,

held high, hoisted, soldier by soldier, over the dogs,
the ropes, and gently set down.
Now he's watching as two other men grip my arms,
a club is lifted under my chin,
I'm made to rise—and somehow I'm still
singing. We all are
raising our voices. It's a determined gentleness, a whisper
that carries. Justin can't look away.
This is the first time he's ever seen men hurt each other.
Have we planned this,
our voices held to a soft timbre,
a punishing tenderness,
the television cameras on the soldiers and the children?
Nothing the young man can say comforts
my son who's crying, who refuses
to look away. This soldier can't be much older
than nineteen. His heavy riot gear
seems too big for him—like wings
he could never lift. He presses down
on a dry leaf under his boot's toe
not to make it crumble
but just to feel the spring to it, the little creaking
as it gives. And now he gazes at my son
as if this eight year old were the only safe place
for his eyes to fall.

Secondary Boycott

Today a woman insists her sons must eat grapes.
Alone I've been walking an eccentric circle
before the store, asking people
not to buy fruit in this A&P. "There's blood
on those grapes," I whisper to her back.
Then a man comes out, sucking the skin
off a grape, mocking me,
shouting in front of his three thin, nervous children.

Now I understand a sniper's need
to hurt someone, to carry rage to its lofty heights.
All afternoon I have criminal hungers.
I am a wave that pushes
in front of everyone, tries to break
against each shopper, even the elderly man
from the Friends' Home. Why can't I let him be?
he wants to know. It's too far
for him to walk to the next market.

But finally he listens,
even blesses me,
shakes my hand so extravagantly
the manager comes out of the door
only to be scolded off by a cane and trembling fingers.
We showed him, we showed that bugger.
The old man salutes, his last word perching in the air
like a large, black sea-fowl
impossibly far inland,
on a rainspout, preening its feathers,
and for a long time afterward
I scurry from shopper to shopper, spilling secrets
like a shorebird
in a strange and trusting music:

boycott, boycott, boycott, boycott, boycott, boycott, boycott.

First Aid at 4 A.M.

In the one light on
in the house, he is choking,
he is banging on the kitchen counter to call his family down
from sleep. He holds his throat,
sinks to his knees.
The cats circle around him, meowing,
waiting to be fed.
How odd it seems.
Two weeks ago he nearly drove a car full of children into
another car. To die on the way to *Pinocchio*?
To choke to death on aspirin?
Then his thirteen-year-old's arms are reaching around him
from the back—they are astonishingly strong.
He feels the child's angry sobs
against his own weakening body,
the boy shouting, "Breathe, damn you,
breathe, daddy,"
the boy half-saving his father,
half-hanging on to him.

The Medical Center for the Aging

Today I teach the class about metaphor.
Imagine you have wings, I tell them, feathers.
Lift, I whisper to Dr. Fernald,
to the retired headmistress Eve Briscoe,
to the frail pianist Eleanor Conwyn, to Idwell Robinson
who, in 1913,
was the champion of all the British Isles.
Where is the wind carrying you?
What do you see below?
I stand behind Mr. Paxton, rub his shoulders.
Imagine wings there,
you are soaring. How does it feel?
Scared, Isabel Pfeiffer says,
who once raised five million dollars for a girls' academy.
Embarrassed, Professor Railsback answers.
Why, swimming, I've always loved swimming, adds Mrs. Behn.
Nervous, insecure, apprehensive, lonely,
come the other answers. *No, no, exhilarated*
insists Mrs. Carduso. *I'm rising.*
This is how wide my wingspan is,
she laughs, spreading out her arms.
I'm casting shadows on the ground—
little children are scared at first when they see me,
they think I'm some sort of prehistoric bird who's escaped
from a museum. We fly over mountains,
rivers, back to each person's home. I make each name the town,
the street. Then we lift away to Tangiers, then return
by way of Reading, Allentown, Pipersville,
and circle over the Medical Center
where all the doctors and nurses rush out, gazing up,
pointing, shaking their fingers.
Come down. Be reasonable. Come down this instant.
Mrs. Carduso wants to fly on
straight into the light, to get so close to the sun
it singes her feathers, and then to plummet.
She catches my arm
tightly and I almost cry out, her fingernails pressing
through the sleeves into my skin,

but I make myself not flinch.
I hold onto the pain. She's got me dangling high over the earth.
I can see how far I'd fall
if she'd loosen her grip.

Exploratory Surgery

Peter would sit at the kitchen table,
that thin, gentle, complaining man,
and find fault with his students, the rain or lack of it, his geese.
How well he and those birds understood each other,
always underfoot,
on each other's property, hissing,
going off in huffs, turning back
to scold. He used to tell us with sweet reasonableness
how soon he and Daniel would have down pillows,
pate de foie gras.
Recipes for Confit d'Oie, Gaensklur,
roasted goose with ginger and pearl onions,
goose livers cooked in dry sherry
got mixed with English Comp. essays and returned to students.
Oh, he'd smother them,
he'd wring the squawks and preenings out of them.

Peter had insisted
he could drive himself to the hospital.
Didn't we think he could do anything on his own now?
Hadn't Daniel better stay home
and do the dishes he'd let pile up,
finally get to the weeds as he'd been promising Peter,
fix the loose step before one of them killed himself on it?

Two hours after Peter had left,
Daniel had come upon the truck, a few miles down the road,
the engine still running,
Peter's stocking cap snarled on a branch,
on the path tinfoil wrappings
of those peppermint lifesavers Peter liked to suck
to help himself recover from a meal
or a lecture he'd found insufferable, both of which,
he'd always add, he'd prepared himself.
Peter leaving litter,
who'd scold us if we ground out a cigarette
in the woods, who'd make us beep the horn
if someone in the car in front of us threw out trash.

This was a man who used to need someone along to explain
why he was charging across
another man's property, a walking stick raised like a sword,
his raincoat flapping behind him.
Once he had leaped into the gunsight of a hunter,
once he blundered into underbrush and two naked teenagers.

When finally Daniel found his friend in the dry creekbed,
when he'd bent down to touch Peter's cheek,
he hadn't been sure if he was still alive.
But Peter had sighed, stood up,
had shaken the leaves off himself. He'd known
you can't walk off and leave the engine running,
your overnight bag on the seat,
you can't just lie down and listen
to the trunks of the skinny trees brushing against each other
at the creek's edge. You can't just let the leaves cover you,
the night sift over you,
you can't spread out your arms and pull it against you,
lift it in great soft handfuls over you,
pack it against you, cold, firm.
There are those who depend upon you,
you have to let them help you,
you have to go on bitching and teasing and quarreling
as your friends expect you to.
There are still papers to be signed,
the slow tedious chore of dying left to be done.

The Death of a Color

Waiting for Steven to bring the body home,
you move through the farmhouse
as if these rooms were now underwater,
as if the sun couldn't reach down here,
the light couldn't insist
on thistle, sweet lavender, gentian, teal blue.
Your son is dead, and it seems a color
has been removed from the world.

You go through his bureau drawers:
a safety patrol badge, six blue shirts all alike,
a ropebelt, extra shoelaces,
a small tin of sugared grapefruit slices still unopened,
underwear, condoms hidden inside a rolled pair of socks.
Now without that clumsy body
to imagine the rubbers hidden for,
they're grotesque, colorless and naked as sea-worms.
How can you endure even the next hour?

You look down,
there's salt on your damp, open palm. How long
have you been feasting on little heaps of salt?
You mouth is dry and musty,
its roof arches,
it's a ribbed, receding cave,
it's a tunnel that falls away.
How have you ever been able to speak,
the words rise out of this black throat?

Look what your hands are doing now.
They're not to be trusted.
Wanting a drink, you find yourself at the window,
no glass in your hand,
just the ice cubes melting there.
You squeeze silver, penetrating cold,
making it spread from the center of your palm,
through the small bones of your wrist,
up your arms.

This is better,
better than pure, blank space
and you floating on it.
You clutch the ice,
the pain grips you, it does not let you go.
It holds you there—for now.
It will not let you go.

Vacation Bible School

My five year olds and I lift Jesus
off and on the cross.
Impossible as a god,
he's great as a doll,
there's pleasure in slipping his legs
through their straps, looping his arms
over the hooks, hanging him just so,
getting him right.

The bread of heaven?
the cup of salvation?
All afternoon the children and I make apostles out of dough,
baptize saints—
too much water and the edges soften, fall away.
Behind us in the church hall, the Red Cross
are unloading padded tables,
doughnuts, juice, clear plastic sacs.
As a boy I went with my father to the Bloodmobile once
and was sure I'd be strapped down,
I'd be forgotten there by my father, by everyone,
and the blood would be left to drain
from my body. Can he sip all his blood out of him
through this small cut
that's opened again on his thumb,
Glenn wants to know—all his many rivers?

And I tell him and Sarah, Craig
and Alisha, Kathleen and Justin and Amanda
that when I was a kid their age
my friends and I called our blood *shadow stuff*.
Our shadows were blood and we tried
to walk ahead of them,
to step out of their dark reach.

I am forty-six now, a father,
a teacher. Nothing convinces me
there's any life but this.
Yet how can I imagine these children dead forever,

unshriven dust?

Today the church's sanctuary is as cool
as a grape arbor. In our pew
Kathleen lifts the pale blues and crimsons off the sill
of a stained glass window, spills them
out of her cupped hands.
Then she goes with me to the altar
to drink the wine.

And I who love
the way one word vanishes into another
like water into sand,
kneel with her at the railing and then it's my turn
and I am drinking a shadow,
your shadow, Jesus.

Site 29, Santiago

There are small mounds of the dead at Site 29
where men have shoveled dirt
over the children's bodies as they might to put out a fire.
Tonight we search for the most searing words,
spit them out
as if flames we might seal in envelopes,
send so that men—prison commandants, military governors—
might open them, flinch
trying to shake the burning from their fingers.
But there are strict rules to these letters,
we have to write them carefully, our backs bent
over the words as if by protecting them
we might also shield the women for whom we ask mercy,
beg release. The letters written,
we lie down, this evening, relearning each other's weaknesses,
the shy eagerness to the nipples,
the tiny, humble stitches of the anus.
In a cell's blue light a boy is dragged over the floor,
one leg twitching,
an eye already torn from its socket,
and the men ask Marte Villez, *Is this your son?*
Is this your sweet son?
My darling, we lie down, searching for the consoling smoothness
of each other's thighs, the soft animal parts
carrying on their own blind lives without us,
our legs, complacent serpents
looped over one another in their dark, ambiguous places.
In a world where a man disappears,
is "disappeared"—
even the grammar twisted and frightening—
how is it we lie down, this night?

One More Christmas Pageant

As I wrap the thongs around my son's legs,
strap the cord at his waist,
tighten his robe around him, rubbing its silver fur,
sending him out into the scents of wax and pine,
I think it could almost be me
who's to follow, the child stepping out
years before into the candlelit dark
of First Parish, Unitarian, the last of the magii
in my parents' church built on the faith
there was no Son of God,
only a good man we sang hymns to.
As a boy I'd secretly hoped there'd be more to Christmas,
some grace, a gift freely given,
more standing between me and evil, me and death,
than a few earnest men.

I took slow, processional steps down the center aisle
to the manger and the baby Jesus
placing before him a sandalwood box
filled with buttons I'd saved, lead soldiers, lucky pennies,
red and blue sea-glass I'd chipped into gems,
proud—for once in my life—of my sacrifice,
this fabulous generosity.

Swimming Lessons in England

Tonight the water's deeper than any my son's ever swum,
the pool so clear that even from this windowed balcony
where I sit with the other parents, watching,
I can see the scratches at its bottom,
my son at his lessons
in a country we've come to live in only this month.
Justin sinks, makes his weight go to the soles of his feet,
forcing himself to drop further down each time.
He's shy, it's been hard for him to make friends
though finally he has. Tonight
at pool's edge, the three of them
do the kind of skipping step boys do
when told not to run,
their thin bodies brushing. I'd forgotten
how fragile an eleven-year-old can be,
his skin rippled when he lifts an arm.
Now when he looks up to the balcony where I am,
the light flashes off the water, and he can't see me,
but still he raises his hand slightly
as if merely stretching,
the kind of wave a boy gives when he doesn't want to be seen
waving—but needs to, needs someone there
who understands how brave he is.
I could bear to die if death were like this,
were only distance. From a balcony,
from the high, hard seat reserved me,
to see this boy glancing up,
not sure if his father's watching,
but who, smiling and lifting his hand shyly,
chooses to believe I am

Acceptance Speech

How many of us pretend to be bored, press a hand
lightly over the mouth, yawn
while secretly hoping,
in those few seconds it takes for an envelope to be opened,
it will be our names called,
even though we're miles away, un-nominated,
unheralded in our pajamas?

Haven't we wanted all eyes on us,
to be recognized at last
for our small acts of bravery,
members of the Academy having mysteriously known of us?

What if it really happened?
We could indulge ourselves, take a chance,
be joyous,
stand in front of the cameras, calling out names one by one,
Joan Ryan, Terry Henrich, Sharon Owens, Wendy Welter,
making the world acknowledge
no life is ordinary,
it is fed by many rivers, many dark rains.

Pamela Perkins-Frederick, Janine Cole,
Alice Vandegrift, Elizabeth McCarthy, Marjorie Rankin,
Catherine Irwin Bursk,
Mary Ann Adzarito Bursk, Katherine Adzarito.
Whom can I leave off my list to be thanked?

Who has not longed for such a public occasion
to honor those who've refused to submit to despair
or in their despair have grown stronger?
Women who, grieving, have learned a language
that is clear, fierce, and loving:
Gloria Del Vecchio, Elizabeth Young, Deborah Bennett,

Charlotte McGurty Smith, Beverly Stoughton,
Doris Sivel, Colene George,
Carol Hitchen, Inge Leonard, Helen Lawton Wilson,
Nina Griscom, Betty Visser, Marti Padilla

as if saying each name
I could cup water in my palms and offer it to you,
not have it spill through my fingers,
through yours.

Shit

Damnit all to hell,
my father roamed the house, Sundays, looking for a hammer.
On the seventh day he couldn't rest
but had to fix things. *Damn*
was the word grown-ups were supposed to use
if they swore in front of kids.
Bitch, bitch, that's all my boss ever does.
My brother was allowed to use the verb.
It seemed like an old jalopy he'd bought with his own money,
had souped up. It left gravel spinning.
Bitch. I whispered the word so often to myself
once it slipped out at the dinner-table
and I was slapped, was righteously indignant.
It was the dog, only the dog I meant,
Mother. It was *you,*
I said under my breath. How did everything turn crazy on me
all at once, my parents' voices harsh,
accusing. Everyone wanted something from me
I couldn't give, they had no right to keep me at home
and go on demanding it of me.
Assholes, cunts.
Cunt was the word of someone who'd just as soon kill a person
as go for a ride. Fuck them all.
Fuck. How at seventeen had I lived without such a word?
Like a car only I had the keys for in the house.
Fucking shit.

I can almost pinpoint the day I began to depend
on this last curse. *Shit,* I'd say
waking to the baby's cry and it'd actually be shit,
sweet, yellow, clayey. I'd peel it off her bottom.
Now my daughter is eleven and moody as a candle,
as alert, a paradox of tallow
and flame, melting and burning. Hurt in school
she's pulled all her blankets off her bed
and cried herself to sleep on the floor.
And in class today, a student not much older than Nora
tells us how she leads her younger sisters and brother into a closet

and plays them *U-2* and *Platinum Blonde* and *Sheila E,*
gets them to sing along
so they don't hear the full impact
of their mother's head against the wall, their father's
slamming it there again, again.
Then a boy's talking, he says it's his fault
his brother died, he hadn't told his parents about the tapes
he'd overheard, he'd been sworn by his brother
to say nothing of the needle
he'd found in the drawer. *Shit.*
By the windowsill a boy is rubbing his forehead hard,
to the left a girl is looking away.
Shit. Not as in: I'm not going to take anymore of your shit.
Not as in: I don't give a shit.
But *Shit*—like when there's a sob in your throat
and there are kids actually crying in the room
and you don't know how you are going to go on teaching
if the students are going to be this honest, this tender
and the moment's so beautiful and scary
you have to fuck it up.

After Being by Myself All Day

Afterwards I need to sit at a table
near two women talking quietly,
to have their voices
comfort me without their knowing it.
How many gifts never intended for you
do you receive?

Having been alone, I welcome the rain on the window now,
the loneliness of another person,
an elderly woman straightening a cloth
around the circle of her table,
her hand as if by long practice finding the center,
setting there salt and pepper,
the sugar between.

After having whispered to myself all day
I need other words now,
the conversation at the table close by,
one going on outside: rain on metal,
one part of the world talking to another.

Prayer

God of the feather rubbed across a cheek,
God of the tuft of fur under a cat's chin,
finger moistened and pressed into the ear's hollow,
cluck of tongue making hoofbeats, all
brisk, clear sounds listened for
that fit the ear,
folds and wrinkles,
God of lucky alignments,
God of the condom a thirteen-year-old
rolls and unrolls on his thumb.

God of tongue and groove, bevel, slide rule,
slip-knot, paperclip, the bolt's threads—
God of pipes and plugs, tumblers in a lock—

It feels like a nail is being driven
into my skull, she cried out. *My head hurts.*
A gentle woman's brain is dead,
then her body too—
death fitting tight as those middle years of marriage,
as the ring she tugged at, that pushed against
the hard bone of her knuckle.

We stand at the grave
and try to make our feet
fill the prints dried there in the mud.

Surely there is no god of pain and disease,
only some lesser, propitiary one
we can pray to, God of nut and bolt,
safety-pin and rubberband, God of latch and key,
sleeve and gentle tugging there,
God of the hand on the inner arm,
God of a whispered urgency, two friends at a table
talking over the sound of rain,
God of long vowels that linger in our mouths,
whose look we've come to love:
moon, piano, spider, sieve. A language

that is often just a solace to say:
cinammon and *orange, seam* and *wrinkle.*

God of such beautiful approximations,
a saying *yes,* that will have to do,
to see it, feel it. *Yes,*
that will do.

A Note about the Author

Christopher Bursk was born in Cohasset, Massachusetts, and educated at Tufts University and Boston University. He has been the recipient of a Guggenheim Foundation Fellowship and a National Endowment for the Arts Creative Writing Fellowship, and his poems have appeared in *Poetry, The American Poetry Review, Paris Review, Encounter, Manhattan Review,* and elsewhere. He is author of two previous books, *Standing Watch* (Houghton Mifflin, 1978) and *Little Harbor* (Quarterly Review of Literature, 1982) and two chapbooks, *Place of Residence* (Sparrow Press, 1983) and *Making Wings* (State Street Press, 1983). He is married to Mary Ann Bursk, a children's librarian, and has three children, Christian, Nora, and Justin. He lives in Langhorne Manor, Pennsylvania, and teaches at Bucks County Community College.